HONEY, THE CARPET NEEDS WEEDING AGAIN!

DATE DUE

Honey, The Carpet Needs Weeding Again!

It's All in How You Look—and Laugh—at It

Martha Bolton

Servant Publications
Ann Arbor, Michigan

Vine Books is an imprint of Servant Publications
especially designed to serve evangelical Christians.

Published by Servant Publications
P.O. Box 8617
Ann Arbor, Michigan 48107

Cover design by Multnomah Graphics and Printing
Cover illustration by Mike Lester
Interior illustrations by Gerald L. Gawronski/ The Look

94 95 96 97 10 9 8 7 6 5 4 3

Printed in the United States of America
ISBN 0-89283-798-5

Library of Congress Cataloging-in-Publication Data

Bolton, Martha, 1951–
  Honey, the carpet needs weeding again : it's all in how
  you look—and laugh—at it / Martha Bolton
  135p. cm
  ISBN 0-89283-798-5
    1. Christian life—Humor. 2. Christian life—Anecdotes.
  3. American wit and humor. 4. Bolton, Martha, 1951–
  I. Title.
BV4517.B64 1993
248.4'0207 dc-20   93-42704

Dedication

To Ann, Andy, and Andrew Joseph
for your friendship,
your example of faith,
and your love of laughter.

Contents

Acknowledgments

A special thank you to:

My husband, Russ,
who never pursued his dream of becoming an archae-
ologist. He says he doesn't regret it, though. He figures
that with my housekeeping, he's performed just as
many excavations and inhaled as much dust as he
would have anyway.

My sons, Rusty, Matt, and Tony,
who grew up thinking all families have char-broiled
gelatin for dessert.

To Liz Heaney, Ann Spangler, and Beth Feia,
who never pushed me too hard to meet my deadlines.
(I'm sure they were just kidding about taking my first-
born hostage.)

And to all of you who have stood in my autograph
lines to get one of my books. I really appreciate it. And
I'd say that even if you weren't my relatives.

Introduction

THE BIBLE said it thousands of years ago and modern day science agrees—laughter is good medicine. It's a salve for the wounded spirit and one of the most effective antidepressants around. It doesn't come with a doctor's bill, it's easy to swallow, and you can have as many refills as you want.

So, when life's little frustrations come your way, give yourself a healthy dose of laughter. It's the perfect prescription for us all.

Martha Bolton
1993

Been There—
Learned That

I'VE LEARNED my share of lessons in life, such as:

- A three-minute egg doesn't need to boil for two-and-a-half hours. Two hours is plenty.

- When the dust settles, most of it will land on my coffee table.

- It's easy to follow the crowd... unless they're all doing advanced aerobics.

- Silence is golden... especially if it's time for my solo at church on Sunday morning.

- He who hesitates has probably just had his son ask for his first driving lesson.

- Burning your candle at both ends will only make your birthday cake taste smokey.

- A bird in the hand makes for a very lumpy handshake.

- A stitch in time saves nine... especially if you're on your third plate at an all-you-can-eat buffet.

- It's never a good idea to tailgate a police car.

- If at first you don't succeed, you're probably trying to assemble an item marked "easy assembly."

- There are three things in life you can count on: death, taxes, and a car alarm going off accidentally at two o'clock in the morning.

- All work and no play will earn you a raise... in your blood pressure.

- When the going gets tough, you're probably trying to cut through one of my steaks.

- The best laid plans of mice and men will always be the ones you forgot to save before turning off your computer.

- The early bird may get the worm, but corn flakes taste a lot better.

- The shortest distance between two points will never be the one a before-dinner speaker takes when you're famished.

- You should take time every day to stop and smell the roses. At sixty bucks a dozen, who can afford to buy them anymore?

- Two heads are better than one, but they can sure make your turtleneck fit a little snug.

- The quickest way to a man's heart is through his stomach. (I know this to be true because my husband says it takes less than forty-five seconds for my cooking to give him heartburn.)

But the most important thing I've learned in life is that faith in God and a healthy sense of humor can get you through even the most trying of times. It's all in how you look... and laugh... at it.

The Great Pew
Invasion

I NOTICED IT THE MINUTE I walked into the sanctuary that Sunday, but by then it was too late. There wasn't a thing I could do about it. My heart began to pound, my knees wobbled, and I broke into a cold sweat and started hyperventilating.

Someone was sitting in my pew.

Okay, so it wasn't *really* my pew. I didn't pay for it or anything like that. It didn't have my nameplate on it. (It used to, but the ushers made me take it down.)

Still, it was *my* pew. Everyone knew it was my pew. It was where I always sat—third row from the back on the left-hand side.

The Phillips family sat in the third row from the back on the right-hand side. I'd never dream of sitting in their pew. Not again, anyway. I tried that once, but as soon as the pastor asked the congregation to stand, the Phillips slid in behind me and forced me to relocate. (Unfortunately, this sort of pew-jacking is quite common in many churches.)

The Randolph family had homesteaded the front row, center section, and they didn't take any chances. Each and every Sunday they'd arrive at church an hour early just to rope off their pew. That in itself may sound reasonable, but I still say those security guards they posted at each end were a bit much.

Mr. Carter claimed the fourth row from the front, right-hand section, aisle seat. Once, an usher tried to persuade him to scoot down in order to leave room for latecomers, but he merely took out his wallet and produced pictures of his father sitting in that seat, his grandfather sitting in that seat, and his great-grandfather sitting in that seat. The way he figured it, that seat was a family heirloom, and he wasn't about to give it up.

The above cases may sound extreme, but if you've studied Pew Theory as I have (I did my thesis on it), you'll find pew possessiveness is not unusual. Thousands of regular church attendees have their chosen pews—pews which took weeks, months, perhaps even years to stake out.

Selecting the family pew is no simple undertaking. The perfect pew must have the perfect location. If you happen to select a pew that's under a heating duct, you could find yourself breaking out into a sweat even when the pastor *isn't* preaching on tithing. But you don't want it under an air conditioning vent either, or icicles could start forming on your hymnal and the membership might think you're a little strange for keeping your choir robe on throughout the entire service.

Another consideration in pew selection is the cushion. It needs to have just the right "give." Surveys have shown that the ideal pew cushion is one which would allow you to sit tall when the pastor is praising the congregation on their faithfulness but to sink down three or four inches when he begins the building fund pledge drive.

However, a pew cushion that's too soft and comfortable may not be a good idea. Halfway through the service, you could become drowsy, lose your mental alertness, and end up volunteering to be the church newsletter editor, serve as youth camp counselor, and teach the three-year-olds' Sunday School class—all with one yawn and the inadvertent stretching of your arm upward.

I had considered all these points when I made my pew selection. My pew of choice wasn't too soft or too hard. It wasn't too hot or too cold. It was perfect. But now, all I could do was stand by helplessly while someone was shamelessly trespassing—invading my territory, jumping my claim.

Seeing the disbelief on my face and fearing I might faint from the shock, an usher quickly led me to the tenth row, center section.

"It'll be all right," he smiled, patting my hand reassuringly. "Maybe you'll get your favorite pew back next week."

Wait a minute, I thought to myself. Next week? My pew wasn't on a time-share program. It had been my pew every Sunday as long as I could remember. There wasn't any room for compromise here.

"Come on, cheer up," he continued, handing me a Sunday bulletin. "Who knows? You may end up liking this pew even better."

Obviously, he didn't understand. I couldn't forget my old pew that easily. That pew and I had been through a lot together. It had been there for me through the ups and downs of the song services. It had endured all of my fidgeting during those annual stewardship sermons. It had heard every prayer I had prayed and had absorbed every tear I had cried. It knew me and I knew it. I knew the exact location of each loose thread in the upholstery. I had memorized the pattern of the nicks in the wood trim. There was no way I could turn my back on it now.

I pouted during the announcements and gritted my teeth while the congregation sang "I Surrender All." I tried singing along, but I couldn't. I was afraid my "all" might include my pew, and I wasn't sure I was ready for such a sacrifice.

Somehow, though, by the close of the service that sacrifice didn't seem so great. To my amazement, I discovered that my new pew was every bit as comfortable as my old one and even had something my former pew didn't have—a brand new family who had been wanting to become more involved in the church. I had the opportunity to meet them and encourage them to attend some upcoming events.

The following Sunday the ushers once again filled my old pew, forcing me to sit in the eighth row, left-hand section. There, I met a lady who was going through a difficult situation similar to one I had faced a few years earlier. I was able to get to know her as well and tell her about the reality of God's faithfulness and love.

After a few more Sundays away from my pew, it no longer mattered where I sat—in the front, in the back, on the right side, or left side. I enjoyed every pew. They were all a part of God's house, and one wasn't any better than the next.

Now granted, you won't see The Great Pew Invasion mentioned in the history books, and the subject doesn't come up much at the Pentagon, but it was an important event in my life.

Now, when the ushers ask me to scoot down a few seats, instead of digging in my heels and singing "I Shall Not Be Moved," I look them right in the eye and sing "I'll Go Where You Want Me to Go."

These Changing Times

A LOT OF THINGS have changed over the years. It used to be the only people shopping at two o'clock in the morning were burglars. Not anymore. Television shopping channels have introduced the concept and convenience of twenty-four-hour spending. No longer do you have to wait for the malls to open. Now, you can sink hopelessly into debt in the privacy of your own home, and you can do it any time of the day or night. Yes, gone are the good ol' days when staying up late to watch TV only cost you your sleep. Today, it can cost a small fortune as you shop 'til you drop... the remote, that is.

The advantages to home shopping are clear. For one thing, you don't have to worry about finding a place to park. If you're busy watching television, chances are your son's already borrowed the car, anyway.

You don't even have to deal with rude and irate customers. When you do all your shopping at home, the only thing that might blow a fuse is your television set... and maybe your husband when the credit card statements start arriving in the mail.

Our shopping habits aren't the only ones that have changed. We've altered the way we do our banking as well. Today, most banking needs can easily be handled over the telephone. By simply pressing the proper numbers on my touch-tone phone, I've transferred funds from one account to another, inquired about the status of a missing check, and found out my savings account balance. (It's the first time I've ever heard a computer laugh.)

You need to be careful when banking by telephone, though. The other day I misdialed and spent twenty minutes trying to get a grandmother in Des Moines to tell me what my last six debits were.

The way we get our junk mail has even changed. Since the invention of the fax machine, companies no longer have to wait the customary three or four mailing days to start irritating us with their unsolicited advertisements. Now, they can do it instantly using our faxes and our paper. I don't know about you, but I don't need a bunch of junk mail tying up my telephone line for hours on end. I've got a seventeen-year-old for that.

We've changed the way we get in touch with each other, too. These days, virtually everyone wears a beeper—doctors, lawyers, even the toddler next door. Last Sunday, we had beepers going off in every corner of our church. It could have been very disruptive, but luckily the congregation just thought it was some sort of new bell choir and applauded.

The most aggravating change of all, though, has to be the gradual phasing out of the real live operator. More and more businesses are using automated answering systems now. They're becoming so popular, I'm afraid one of these days I'm going to call a church only to be greeted by the following:

"Hello. You've reached First Church of the Nineties. For faster service, please press the following numbers on your touch-tone telephone:

"For a schedule of our services, press 1.

"Desire a visit from the ministerial staff? Press 2.

"If you're in need of more faith, press 3 and try to believe someone will be with you shortly.

"Want more joy in your life? Press 4 for a recording of our pastor's best sermon anecdotes.

"Need to learn to be more long-suffering? Press 5 for a recording of our pastor's worst sermon anecdotes.

"Having trouble making decisions? Press 6. Uh, maybe you'd better make that 7. No, on second thought, go ahead and press 6... unless you truly believe 7 would be better.

"If you think too much gossip goes on in our church, press 8 and tell us what you've heard. Speak clearly and be sure not to leave out a single detail!

"Feel like no one has time for you? Press 9.... Sorry, all those lines are busy at the moment. Please hang up and try your call again later."

Whether it's for better or worse, life is full of change... except the kind you used to get back at the grocery store.

I Brake for Walls

B UMPER STICKERS are wonderful. Not only can they cover any dings which your automobile has sustained over the years, but they also give other drivers something to do while tailgating you on the freeway.

There are funny bumper stickers, thought-provoking bumper stickers, and bumper stickers for both noble and ridiculous causes. There are wordy bumper stickers and wordless bumper stickers. There are as many different bumper stickers as there are drivers on the road today.

Some bumper stickers make statements about the car: "So many stop signs, so little brakes." Or "This car is a collectible—it collects dirt in the carburetor, nails in the tires, and dents in the body work."

Other bumper stickers make statements about the driver. For instance, "I brake whenever my wife tells me to" or "How am I driving? Beats me. I don't even have a license!"

A few bumper stickers reveal the driver's financial status. For instance, "My other car was repo'ed," or "I owe. I owe. Where did my rebate go?" I also like the "Don't laugh—this wreck's paid for (although I'm still making payments on the gasoline!)" bumper sticker.

Some folks use their bumpers as a forum to brag about their children. We've all seen these bumper stickers. They say things such as "My daughter sits next to an honor student at Fremont High" or "My son made the Dean's list! (Typed it, that is.)"

Instructional bumper stickers are the ones which tell other drivers what to do, like "Honk, if you enjoy irritating others," or "Don't tailgate. I just might be your pastor!"

There are even bumper stickers with spiritual messages. For instance, "Pray for rain. It's cheaper than a car wash."

I try to stay away from bumper stickers that date the driver. That's why last week I finally removed my "Vote for Lincoln" and "I survived the Ice Age" bumper sticker.

Often a bumper sticker is used to air the driver's complaints, such as "My boyfriend went to Alaska and all he brought back for me was a cold shoulder!" or "I got a call from my daughter's school, a letter from the IRS, my plumbing stopped up, and my in-laws just moved in with me. How's your day going?"

Other bumper stickers try to convince the world to be more ecologically minded: "Keep America beautiful—never open a teenager's closet!"

My favorites, though, are the glow-in-the-dark bumper stickers. These come in handy when it's late at night and you're trying to find your car in a mall parking lot.

Bumper stickers can even be used to protect a vehicle from would-be car thieves. I mean, who in their right mind would steal a car that's sporting a "This car is protected by nuclear warheads. Have a nice day" bumper sticker?

Favorite vacation spots can also be a topic for fender messages, like the ever-popular "I ♥ Siberia" and those "I hiked the lunar craters" bumper stickers.

Bumper stickers come in many different sizes. Some are so small, you can't read them even if you're pushing the car. Others are too big for the vehicle. I saw a sub-compact once with a sticker that said, "Have a nice... (continued on front bumper)."

Last but not least are political bumper stickers. Every election year we see bumper stickers for the Democratic candidates, the Republican candidates, the Independent candidates, and whoever else has thrown his or her hat into the ring. Have you noticed how political bumper stickers tend to stick long after the election is over. Now if we could just get all those campaign promises written on them to do the same thing!

Make Nothing
from Something

CREATIVE PEOPLE impress me. People who can make something out of nothing. People who can turn leftover swatches of material into a beautiful quilt, or build a stately bookcase from mere scrap lumber.

I'm not like that at all. The only thing I can make

out of scrap lumber is a bonfire. I'm the type of person who makes nothing out of something.

Allow me to illustrate my point.

I once made a trivet out of Popsicle sticks. It turned out nice, but got pretty messy when all the Popsicles started to melt.

Then, there was that throw rug that I made. I know it was a throw rug because as soon as my family saw it, they wanted to throw it.

Making my own clothes isn't my thing either. I always seem to have trouble with the darts. Oh, I can usually get the darts to hit the garment, but I can never remember if it's the pocket that's worth fifty points or the collar.

I even tried knitting my own sweater out of wool. But it turned out so ugly, the sheep demanded it back.

Next, I tried needlepoint. But it was my finger that usually got it... the needlepoint, that is. I had to give up that craft by doctor's orders. He said the blood loss was making me anemic.

Then, there was the entertainment center which I built with my very own hands. I have to admit it was great having my television set, my stereo, my VCR, my CDs and my videos all in one place—a pile in the middle of my living room floor after the shelves collapsed.

My father was creative. He could take whatever lumber he had lying around the garage and create furniture that would rival pieces found in the finest department stores. Bookcases, coffee tables, decorator shelves—Dad could make anything.

Once, he even made his own Christmas tree. I'm not talking about the artificial kind you simply take out of a box and put together either. My father actually *made* his own tree. He drilled holes in an old broom handle, then inserted hedge branches of varying lengths into each hole. Believe it or not, it really did look like a Christmas tree (and was quite a conversation piece!)

From helping a neighbor repair a broken fence to building new Sunday School rooms at a local church, my father imposed no limits on his talents. He didn't make excuses if the proper tools or supplies weren't available. He didn't wait for "tomorrow," "sometime," or "one of these days." He refused to let doubt fade his vision or stifle his imagination. Instead of focusing on what he lacked, he simply forged ahead with the talents God had given him and whatever resources he had.

Paper, Plastic, or Crane

NEVER go grocery shopping when you're hungry. When you're hungry, you can smell Oreos from twelve aisles away, see Klondike Bars in the freezer through a crowd of twenty, and actually "taste" the Ding Dongs through both the box and each individual foil wrapping.

Everything in the supermarket will look good to you. You'll find yourself drooling over tofu and licking your lips over the Brussels sprouts. You'll catch yourself asking the store manager if you could go ahead and open that jar of pickled pigs' feet to munch on while you shop.

I know whenever I go shopping when I'm hungry, I end up grabbing everything in sight and tossing it into my cart—chocolate chip cookies, brownies, potato chips and dip, the stockboy... nothing's safe. I fill my cart so full, the Keebler elves on top start getting dizzy from the altitude.

I've also noticed that when I'm hungry, my shopping cart seems to take on a personality of its own. As long as I'm loading it up with all sorts of calorie-laden goodies, it'll behave beautifully. But the minute I try heading for the check-out stand, its wheels lock up. The only way I can get it moving again is to turn it around and aim it in the direction of the Hostess display for just one final pass.

Even when I do finally make it up to the check-out counter, I'm still not home free. I have to pass by shelf after shelf of strategically-placed temptations. It's hard to ignore all the candy bars, chocolate-covered mints and licorice, especially when they're right next to a supermarket tabloid announcing that two-headed aliens have landed in Albuquerque and have opened an accounting service there.

The only thing more damaging to the family budget than grocery shopping when you're hungry is taking a hungry husband with you. Hungry husbands tend to shop like one of those contestants in a free grocery shopping spree, selecting their food items a shelf at a time. Their eyes aren't just bigger than their stomachs, they're bigger than the whole state. If you tell a hungry husband to go get some lunchmeat, he'll come back with three turkeys and a side of beef. Ask him to pick up some snack food and he'll return with the entire Laura Schudder's collection, including display rack and hardware.

Hungry husbands also become more daring in their choices of food items. They'll pick out things they normally wouldn't even touch. When shopping with a hungry husband, it's not uncommon to hear him comment, "Yum, this can of stewed cactus sure looks good," or "What d'ya say we try some of this tripe?"

You'll also find hungry husbands stocking up on sale items. For example, last week my husband purchased eighty-six cans of garbanzo beans. He figures they should last our family about a year... especially since no one in the family even likes them. Besides, he wanted to be prepared in case that garbanzo bean shortage we've heard so much about ever does hit.

Taking hungry teenagers shopping with you isn't

a good idea, either. Not only will they try to get you to buy the whole store, they'll try to convince you to buy the entire chain.

Whenever my teenagers go shopping with me, we end up having to use the "Fifteen carts or less" check-out lane. In fact, after they're done shopping, the store has to be closed down for several hours just to restock the shelves.

Shopping with hungry toddlers is just as bad. It's amazing how many items they can reach from that little seat in the cart. And if they can't reach something, the hungry husband or hungry teenager will gladly give them a boost up to it.

I suppose the bottom line is if you're going to go grocery shopping when your stomach's empty, you'd better make sure your wallet's full!

"We've got to go back in. We forgot the milk and
bread we stopped for in the first place."

Knock, Knock

O PPORTUNITY isn't the only thing you'll hear knocking at your door. Often it's a salesperson. I don't know about you, but at our house, door-to-door salespeople always seem to come at the worst times—like when I'm home. They also like to come when I'm in the middle of cooking dinner. (I think my family pays them to do this.)

I'm sure I get this parade of peddlers because

around town I'm what's known as an easy sell. (I've taken more goods off people's hands than the IRS.) I'll buy anything.

Some of the items I buy are worthwhile. Others are a waste of money... like that $28 marble doorstop I bought the other day. I didn't need that. My meatloaf can perform the same task, and it's free.

I didn't need that canine curling iron I bought last week, either. My dog will hardly sit still for it, and to tell you the truth, he doesn't look all that great in spiral curls anyway.

High-pressure salespeople who won't take no for an answer are the absolute worst. I once had an encyclopedia salesman take so long with his pitch, the set had to be updated four times before he could even sell it. Then, there was that magazine saleswoman who stayed at our house through two Christmases and a family wedding. More often than not I find myself buying something from these salespeople just to get them to leave. This method works, but it can get very expensive if they're realtors.

Some salespeople use the angle that they'll win the trip of a lifetime if only you'll place an order. I generally like to help out in these types of situations. In fact, if they awaken me before eight in the morning, I'm quite happy to see them go as far away as possible.

I get irritated by the frequency of some salesmen's visits. A salesman who paints the street numbers on curbs stops by our house at least once every two months. He has to. With all the earthquakes here in California, that's how often our address changes. Another peddler stops by even more often than that. As a matter of fact, he spends so much time at our house, we had to count him in the last census.

I don't let this steady stream of salespeople get me down, though. That's because after all these years, I've finally discovered a way to make it work in my favor. Once a week I invite a vacuum cleaner salesman to demonstrate how well his upright works on my carpets. Twice a week I let another salesperson show me how well her patented "supermop" performs on my kitchen and bathroom floors. Every Thursday I call a cookware salesman to come over and demonstrate how easy it is to prepare a seven-course meal in his pots and pans. And whenever I'm going out for the evening, I ask the Avon lady if she'd like to stop by and give me a free makeover.

Now, all I'm waiting for is a typewriter salesman to ring my doorbell so I can trick him into answering all my fan mail. (I hope he hurries up, too. That letter should have been answered months ago!)

Carry-All Mom

WHEN I was a little girl, people would ask me what I wanted to be when I grew up. "A shelf" never once occurred to me.

I wonder if anyone has ever calculated how many things a mother ends up holding throughout her lifetime. From diaper bags that outweigh the Rock of Gibraltar to portable playpens, from science fair projects too heavy for a fourth-grader to Little League equipment, a mother's arms have seen it all.

I know whenever my family and I go to an amusement park, I somehow end up carrying everyone's sunglasses, jackets, drinks, and all their souvenirs. Oh, it starts out innocently. My youngest son will ask me to hold his soda while he goes on the roller coaster. Figuring the person sitting behind him probably wouldn't care for a root beer shower, I agree. I'm not going on the ride, anyway. I don't like roller coasters. I get dizzy on a carousel, so why would I chance a roller coaster?

After the ride, though, he'll forget to take his drink back. But that's okay because now he wants to ride it again with his brother.

"Mom," his brother will ask. "Would you mind holding my jacket?"

Before I can answer, they're out of sight and the jacket is in my arms.

My husband and third son now return from their souvenir shopping spree. When they find out the others are on the roller coaster, they, too, want to try it.

"Dear," my husband will say, handing me his sunglasses, a balloon, three stuffed animals, and a souvenir coffee mug. "Can you please hold these until we get back?"

"Sure," I say, then wave good-bye with my one free hand. Noticing it's empty, he hands me his half-eaten ice cream cone.

"They don't allow food on the rides," he explains before rushing off.

At some point throughout the evening, someone will finally notice that the top of my head can no longer be seen over the mountain of gear.

"Hey, where'd Mom go?" my youngest son will ask.

"She was here a minute ago," my husband says, taking the melted ice cream cone from my hand.

Then, one by one, they'll begin retrieving their belongings and eventually find me.

But that's OK. After all, it's not that they're unwilling to carry things for me. My teenagers are always offering to carry my cash, and on numerous occasions my husband has said he'd be more than happy to take our credit cards off my hands.

Foot-Stomping Shopping

WHATEVER happened to the concept of strolling through a department store for a peaceful afternoon of shopping? Nowadays, most stores have their music turned up so loudly, the only thing you want to buy is a good set of earplugs!

Where are those great shops of yesteryear, those

consumer havens where the only heavy metal sounds you heard were the hangers being scooted along the racks and where "rap" was merely something the clerk did to a gift you just bought? The nearest thing those stores had to music videos was "The Lawrence Welk Show" airing on one of the television sets in the electronics department. Back then, no one had even heard of "rhythm shopping." If you saw a customer snapping her fingers, it was just to get her kids to quit climbing on the mannequins. And the only moonwalking you ever saw was when a customer got his heel caught in the escalator.

Actually, I wouldn't mind shopping to music so much if they'd just play better selections. With all the great songs they have to choose from, you'd think they could be a little more creative. For instance...

- When I'm trying to fit my body into a size eight pair of jeans, why don't they play "The Impossible Dream"?

- When two customers start wrestling over the same blouse, a couple of verses of "Let There Be Peace on Earth" seems appropriate.

- When that dress I've been eyeing for months finally goes on sale, how about "What a Difference a Day Made"?

- When I'm trying to figure out how to tell my husband a new dress cost only thirty dollars instead of the fifty that's on its price tag, perhaps "It's a Sin to Tell a Lie" would be a good choice.

- When I'm trying to yank, pull, and stretch a size small pair of Spandex shorts up over my size medium thighs, that's the perfect time for them to be pumping "High Hopes" into the dressing room.

- When dealing with rude clerks or customers, "Try a Little Tenderness" might help ease the tension.

- When my husband is shopping with me and I'm on my twenty-ninth visit to the dressing room, I'm sure he'd appreciate hearing that classic tune, "If It Takes Forever."

- When the salesclerk is running my credit check, "I Say a Little Prayer" might be a nice diversion.

- When I decide to pay cash for my purchases instead and the clerk hands me my change, what better song is there than "Is That All There Is?"

But even this kind of shopping music can be carried too far. When I leave the store and all the alarms go off because the clerk forgot to remove the security tabs from my purchases, I don't really think I want to be serenaded to three verses of "Jailhouse Rock"!

Sitting on the Park Bench, Watching All the Folks Jog By

R ECENTLY MY FRIEND, Linda, suggested the two of us begin a regular walking program. We're both writers and tend to spend a lot of time sitting at the typewriter. That's not to say we're out of shape.

Why, just this morning I lifted seventy-pound weights for ten minutes. (It took me that long to get them off my chest.) And last Tuesday I went roller skating all day. (Actually, I only intended to skate for *one* hour, but I couldn't figure out how to stop.) I do pretty well on my stationary bicycle, too—or at least I thought I did until someone pointed out that the pedals weren't the part that's supposed to stay stationary.

Like most people, though, I don't get all the exercise I need. I should probably spend more time on my rowing machine, but every time I put it in my swimming pool, it sinks. (I'm trying to learn how to hold my breath longer, but so far I haven't been able to get more than one or two pulls on the rows in.) I even went shopping for a treadmill, but I couldn't find one with a "saunter" button.

A walking program, however, sounded like something I could keep up with, so I agreed to give it a try.

We decided to meet every Monday, Wednesday, and Friday morning and walk five or six laps around a local park. I tried changing it to five or six laps around the drinking fountain, but my friend felt we needed to get our blood circulating again. It had stayed sluggish long enough.

Our first lap went fine. We noticed an ambulance circling (someone must have tipped them off), but we refused to let that intimidate us. We even showed off and sprinted once, but unfortunately, the ice cream truck got away.

The third lap was a bit more difficult. Our feet hurt, our legs ached, we were breathing hard and walking so slowly I'm surprised our pedometers didn't clock us at "coma" speed.

By the fifth lap, we were ready to flag down the ambulance, but it had already left on another call.

"How 'bout taking a break?" I pleaded as several seniors effortlessly jogged by. "Let's face it, the park statues are moving faster than we are."

Eyeing a bench off to the side, we made a dash—no, a slow trot—OK, a crawl for it, and sat there the rest of the morning catching our breath.

"You know," Linda said when the color finally returned to our cheeks. "Sitting here watching everyone else walk or jog by isn't helping us any. We're not burning off any calories or working a single muscle in our bodies."

"You're right. You're absolutely right," I said, wiping my brow with my shirt sleeve. "Let's start waving at them, too."

"George prefers low-impact exercises—you know,
like rolling over during a nap."

I ♥ My Pet...
Peeves, That Is

W E ALL HAVE pet peeves—those things that get on our nerves quicker than anything else.

Loud, ear-piercing drive-thru lane microphones are a pet peeve of mine. You know the ones I mean. Their volume is turned up so high, it sends you right through your sun roof (and you don't even have a sun roof!). They're so loud, folks three counties away can hear you order "Two hamburgers, french fries, and a Coke," then hear the clerk repeat "One chicken sandwich, a milk, and a hot apple turnover."

Automated teller machines that run out of cash are another one of my pet peeves. If machines are supposed to be so much smarter than humans, then why is it that they can't hang onto their money any longer than we can?

Tardiness annoys me, too. I'd go into more details about the lack of punctuality in some people and how irritating it can be, but I'm already running late with this manuscript.

Folks who consistently use trite sayings are a major pet peeve for some, but I don't sweat the small stuff. I figure it's no skin off my teeth, so I just go with the flow and let a smile be my umbrella. After all, we all march to a different drummer, so to each his own.

People who call and hang up on my answering machine without saying who they are can be aggravating. Don't they realize I have enough mysteries to solve in my checkbook without having to solve some on my answering machine, too?

Then, there are those who won't let others get a word in edgewise. I know how to take care of folks like that, though. Whenever I'm talking, I don't take a single breath or pause even for the slightest moment. That way, I can be sure that this type of inconsiderate person will never get the chance to monopolize a conversation.

People who think they're always right can grate on you—especially when they won't listen to those of us who really are.

Leaving things to the last minute is another one of my pet peeves. But I'll wait and cover that in the final chapter... if there's still time.

Those who love to exaggerate not only annoy me, but they're a pet peeve of a lot of people. In fact, Queen Elizabeth and I were discussing this very topic the other evening when she and the rest of the royal family stopped by my house for some chip and dip. And when the President called to congratulate me on making the best seller list, he mentioned it as well.

I have to say, though, my biggest pet peeve is people who make lists of their pet peeves. But luckily, I don't know anyone like that.

In Search of Zzzzzs

THE OTHER NIGHT I had a bit of trouble falling asleep. I wasn't at a lecture, studying, or watching a rerun of a television talk show; so naturally, I didn't feel the least bit drowsy. I tossed and turned and ended up staring at the ceiling longer than Michelangelo did in the Sistine Chapel.

I tried everything I could to fall asleep.

I drank a glass of warm milk. All that did was give me an overwhelming desire to sharpen my nails on the carpeting and look under the sofa for mice.

I tried counting sheep, but even they didn't cooperate. Instead of jumping over the fence, they were doing the Hokey Pokey in front of it and I kept losing my count.

Someone once told me that pretending you're being gently rocked to sleep on an ocean liner is a sure cure for insomnia. So I gave this a try. It didn't work either. All I did was worry about how much I should tip the steward.

That's when I decided to watch a little late night television. After flipping through the dial, I settled on the TV test pattern. It seemed to have the best plot of all the movies on at that time of night.

By 3:00 A.M., I was bored with that and still wide awake. I needed something to do. Washing the car would wake up the neighbors, so that was out. I could go grocery shopping, but that didn't sound like much fun. When you're the only one in the store, there's not much point in cart-racing to the sale items.

What I really needed was someone to talk to. Hoping one of the kids might still be awake, I tiptoed down the hall and peeked into their bedrooms. I could hear one of my sons talking in his sleep, so I joined in. Insomniacs do get desperate sometimes.

We had a nice conversation, too, that is, until I asked him about his report card. Then, he suddenly fell into a deep sleep... or at least pretended to.

Desperate for more conversation, I tried to think of someone else who would be up at this hour. Only one answer came to mind—the information operator. I picked up the telephone and dialed. I expected to hear a warm, chipper voice on the other end, but I think I woke her up, too. My first clue was when she answered with, "City, please... and this had better be important!"

At 4:00 A.M. I took my pillow and blanket and tried sleeping on the sofa downstairs. Then, I tried the recliner, and finally, the floor. I watched each second ticking by on the clock. I tried thumbing through a magazine. I did stretching exercises. I took deep breaths. I thought only happy, peaceful thoughts.

I could feel my eyes beginning to get heavy. I yawned a few times. This is it, I thought to myself. At last, I was getting sleepy. Rising to my feet, I made my way upstairs to my bedroom. I crawled into bed, laid my head on my pillow, and closed my weary eyes.

Then, the alarm rang.

The World of
the Naïve

M Y HUSBAND often accuses me of being the most naïve person on earth. He bases this assessment on the fact that I once volunteered to chaperone youth camp so I could rest. (All right, so maybe he does have a point.)

But I'm sure there are others who are just as naïve as I am.

You know you're naïve if...

- You're a parent of teenagers, but you still think that that incoming telephone call is for you.

- You believe that that pitbull with its mouth wrapped around your ankle is really as gentle and friendly as its owner claims.

- You believe the line with three people in it will move faster than the one with twenty-six people in it.

- You're convinced that that policeman who just turned on his red lights and siren behind you is merely testing his equipment.

- You count on a repairman who said he'd be at your home between 8:00 A.M. and 5:00 P.M. to show up sooner than 4:59 P.M.

- You believe you'll find a parking space on your first four trips around the mall.

- You turn down the thermostat and honestly think your wife won't come along in five minutes to turn it back up.

- You think a simple computer billing error will take less than twelve letters and fourteen telephone calls to rectify.

- You believe a speaker's last and final point really is her last and final one.

- But you truly know you're a naïve, trusting soul when you take *two* scoops of my casserole at a church potluck!

14

Get Real!

THESE DAYS, what you see isn't necessarily what you get. We have imitation leather, imitation diamonds, imitation sugar, and imitation butter. There's even imitation bacon. (I think they get it from animals who just act like pigs.)

That succulent turkey featured on the cover of your favorite magazine probably isn't real, either. Chances are you're drooling over nothing more than a raw young Tom that's been plumped up with a stuffing of newspapers and spray painted golden brown. No doubt that corn on the cob next to it has been dyed yellow and brushed with lacquer. And that mouth-watering chocolate layer cake on page 36 is probably nothing more than a waxed model. (And my Thanksgiving Day dinner guests think they've got it rough!)

If you love jogging but hate all the smog, traffic, and muggers, don't worry. You can now exercise in an imitation environment. That's right. You can exercise in the great outdoors without ever leaving the safety and comfort of your own home. All you have to do is play the landscape video of your choice on your big screen television set and hop onto your treadmill, and in an instant you're hiking the Rocky Mountains or taking a brisk evening jog along the beaches of California. (I usually play the emergency room video whenever I exercise. Considering my physical stamina, it just seems more fitting.)

People are becoming less authentic, too. You know the type—they've had their faces lifted, their noses altered, their thighs liposuctioned, their lips enlarged, their tummies tucked, and dimples added to their chins—and they walk into church humming "Just As I Am." (Do you think we need to remind these people that it's love that's supposed to be lifting us, not plastic surgeons?)

I have to admit, though, I've been tempted to have my imperfections surgically corrected, too. I even went to a plastic surgeon for a free consultation. That was six months ago. He's still totaling the estimate.

Some heads of hair may not be what they appear to be, either. But modern hairpieces are so natural-looking, it's difficult to tell who's wearing one and who isn't. I'm sure I never would have known my favorite baseball player was wearing a hairpiece had it not been for that one game when he slid into second and his toupee went on to third.

The other day while I was getting a full set of acrylic nails, I thought to myself how sad it is that people just aren't genuine anymore. I even mentioned it to my dentist when I stopped in to have my caps whitened and to my hairdresser while she was adding a frost to my hair. Later that evening while I was applying another tube of instant tanning cream, I was still thinking about it. What this world needs is more *real* people, I concluded. There are so few of us left.

And the Beat Goes on...
And on... And on

I F YOU EVER say hi to me and I walk by without
acknowledging you, please don't take it person-
ally. I probably still have my earplugs in. I started
wearing them about the same time my son began
taking drum lessons.

Now don't get me wrong. I love waking up to the

sound of crashing cymbals, and that drum roll he plays every time someone enters his room is entertaining, but once in awhile I could use a little of that... what was it called? Oh yeah, peace and quiet.

I'm also concerned about the neighbors. Between my son beating on the drums and those smoke signals coming from my kitchen, who knows what they must be thinking.

I tried talking him into a quieter instrument—like the triangle. I would have let him "ting" on that to his heart's content, but he wouldn't hear of it. Come to think of it, he doesn't hear much of anything over those drums. He doesn't hear me calling him to dinner (at least he *claims* he doesn't). He doesn't hear his father telling him to clean his room. He wouldn't even hear it if someone accidentally drove a car through our living room wall. (I know because when I did that last week, he didn't even look up.) Oddly enough, though, during his practices he hasn't missed a single telephone ring yet.

I have to admit I admire his dedication. He plays those drums every chance he gets. Even when he's not on the drums, he's constantly thinking rhythm, rhythm, rhythm. He'll tap out a beat on anything and everything—the coffee table, his school books, his brother's head.

It's obvious he didn't inherit any of this natural rhythm from me. No matter how hard I try, I just can't seem to keep time. It was hard enough for me to learn to tell it, much less keep any of it. You see, I'm one of the rhythmatically challenged. Whenever I clap to the music in church, I always come in at the wrong time—like during the announcements. But even that's an improvement. At least my hands are meeting now.

Another thing that impresses me is how much coordination playing a drum requires. Until my son began his lessons, I had no idea drums took so much concentration. He'll have his left hand hitting half notes while his right hand is hitting eighth notes and his feet are hitting sixteenth notes. That's not easy—especially hitting those sixteenth notes. The only time I can get my foot moving that fast is during a cramp.

But it takes all those different beats working together to make the best music. It's the same in life, you know. If we're working at an eighth-note pace, we shouldn't be impatient with those who are comfortable with a half-note pace or become discouraged by those who are flying by us at sixteenth-note speed. As long as we are doing our best and staying focused on our own duties and pacing, we can't help but make a symphony together.

*"No, son, your drum practicing doesn't
bother us in the least."*

Weathering It All

C ALIFORNIANS don't get to see a lot of electrical storms. We have to deal with other dangers such as earthquakes, floods, and L.A. freeways.

Midwesterners, on the other hand, know what real lightning is. An electrical storm in Kansas lights up three states. That's why people who travel to middle America should possess basic cloud reading skills. They need to know which clouds mean thunderstorms, which clouds mean possible tornadoes, and which clouds mean the roast should have been taken out of the oven hours ago. I found this out the hard way on a summer trip to my aunt and uncle's home in Arkansas.

From the time we crossed over the California-Arizona border, I watched every cloud with suspicion. I was certain I'd spotted a tornado over Albuquerque, but upon closer scrutiny I realized the cloud was following an airplane and spelling out "Eat at Stuckey's."

Obviously, that was a false alarm, but by the time we arrived in Arkansas, a severe thunderstorm was pounding the area and a tornado watch had been issued.

"A tornado *watch* just means the conditions are right for a tornado," my aunt assured me. "You don't have to worry until a tornado *warning* is issued."

I did not, however, share her confidence. The lightning was putting on its own Fourth of July sky show, the thunder was rattling the windows, and marble-sized hail was pelting the roof. Minutes later, a tornado warning *was* issued.

"Can I worry now?" I screamed, calmly.

She tried explaining that there still was no need for panic. We had plenty of time to get to the storm shelter. Her words of comfort, however, fell on deaf ears—or at least absent ones. I had already grabbed the kids and was sitting in the shelter.

The others soon joined us, and we all sat there in that dark, cement cylinder amidst cobwebs and dust, waiting for the fury of the storm to pass over.

I felt sorry for the children. My middle son, Matt, was too young to grasp the word *tornado*. He thought we were hiding from a "potato" in the sky (an obvious blending of the fear of tornadoes and my cooking).

The other children were equally afraid. But all that screaming and crying "I want to go home! I want to go home!" didn't help matters any. Yet I couldn't stop screaming and crying. I *did* want to go home.

Finally, after what seemed like an eternity, the cloud passed over us, touching down in a field some twenty miles away before heading on toward Memphis.

I was so relieved to be alive that when I stepped out of the shelter I bent over and kissed the ground. That's something we can't do in California. It doesn't stay still long enough.

Honey, The Carpet Needs Weeding Again!

I'M NOT saying what kind of a housekeeper I am, but throughout my entire life no one has ever said to me, "You've made your bed, now lie in it."

All right, maybe I'm exaggerating just a little. I do make my bed, but I don't enjoy it—especially when it comes time to change the sheets. To me, changing sheets seems like a waste of energy. You do it this year, then you've got to turn around and do it again next year, and the year after that. There's just no end to it.

I might not hate changing the sheets so much if it wasn't for that bottom sheet—you know, the "fitted" one which seldom does. The first three corners go on with ease, but getting that last one to stay on requires four people, a crowbar, and plenty of prayer.

Bending the mattress sometimes helps, but you have to be careful. I tried this last week on my son's bed. It worked, but the minute he lay down on it, the far right corner of the sheet snapped off and catapulted him into the hall.

Dishes aren't very high on my list of exciting things to do, either. Luckily, though, my cooking eats through most of my dinnerware, so I hardly ever have any to wash.

Cleaning out my refrigerator is no thrill. Forget the rain forests. If you're really searching for rare and unusual plant life, check out my vegetable drawer. The potatoes in there are beyond the peeling stage. What they need is a good hair stylist. I tell you, you haven't seen anything until you've seen a russet with bangs.

Then, there's my stove. The worst part of cleaning my stove is having to breathe all those fumes—not from oven cleaner but from my cooking spills which have caked on it over the years. From foul fowl to black-bottom pancakes, there's enough dehydrated food there to get a family of four through a brief famine.

When it comes to sweeping, I have to admit I take a few shortcuts. Right now my area rug has so much dirt and debris under it, it looks like a pitcher's mound.

The bathroom is my least favorite room to clean. My tub has modeled more rings than a host on the Home Shopping Network, and the other day I tried for hours to get three streaks out of the medicine cabinet mirror. I finally managed to remove one. (It turned out the other two were on my face.)

Housework may not be fun, but even I realize it's necessary. If you don't want plant life sprouting from your sink, flies sticking to your countertop, or cobwebs so thick your kids can use them for trampolines, there's a certain amount of upkeep that has to be performed on a regular basis.

After all, the proper greeting on our porches should be "Peace to all who enter"—not "Good luck!"

The Sixth Sense—
Your Sense of Humor

ONE OF THE questions I'm asked most often is what's the secret to keeping a good sense of humor while dealing with the ups and downs of everyday living. How can you show that disagreeable person a smile when you'd really rather show him the door? How can you stay encouraged when prices are rising and your paycheck isn't? How do you face those days when everyone you meet got up on the wrong side of the bed, and all you want to do is go back to yours? In short, how can you laugh through your trials?

For one thing, learn to look at the positive. So what if your car has a flat tire (or to be politically correct, I should say an "air deprived tire")? The other three tires aren't flat. Be thankful for that.

An unexpected bill just arrived in the mail? Look on the bright side—at least it didn't come postage due.

They announce your 7:00 P.M. flight's been delayed until 9:00 P.M.? Smile. Your stomach just got a two-hour reprieve before it has to endure airline food.

Stuck downtown in bumper-to-bumper traffic? Look at it this way—normally, people have to pay for downtown parking, and you're getting to do it in the middle of the street for free.

Your dishwasher's overflowing? Don't let that get you down. Just think—you're the first person on your block with a new indoor spa.

Another thing you can do to keep smiling is train yourself to find the humor in your trials. Anyone who looks hard enough, can find some humor in almost every situation.

OK, so your new barber wasn't very good. It

could have been worse. He could have shaved off your *other* eyebrow, too.

Your new puppy just dug up your entire garden? Then quit thinking of him as a puppy. Instead, think of him as a rototiller with a tail.

You just got stuck on the elevator at work? Look at it this way—you finally got that private office you've always wanted.

It's also important that you don't let others determine what your attitude is going to be. Noah didn't let his rude, negative neighbors ruin his day or deter him from accomplishing what he needed to accomplish. He knew they were all wet (or soon would be).

Joseph's brothers threw him down a pit, but he didn't let his attitude stay there. He kept a positive outlook and was eventually able to turn that injustice into something good.

And lastly, try to go through your day with a song in your heart. I know I do. And believe me, it sounds much better staying in there than when it comes out of my mouth!

It's a "Mom" Thing

WE ALL KNOW there's a certain behavior unique to mothers. It defies logic, it's beyond explanation, and there's only one way to describe it: it's a "Mom" thing.

Allow me to give you a little advice.

- When she insists that you put on your overcoat... even after you point out that none of the other kids on the beach are wearing one, don't sweat it. It's a "Mom" thing.

- When you've been a vegetarian for six years and she still doesn't think you're getting enough vegetables in your diet, don't let it chew on you. It's a "Mom" thing.

- When, after slamming on her car brakes, she stretches her hand out in front of you to block your thrust (even though you're safe in your seatbelt), relax. It's a "Mom" thing, and you'll never get her to break it.

- When she still gives you a 10:00 P.M. curfew (which you don't mind, but your wife's getting a little annoyed with it), don't fret. It's just a "Mom" thing.

- When she insists on holding your hand while crossing the street, even though you're needing to hold *your* kids' hands while crossing the street, work it out somehow. It's a "Mom" thing.

- When she has on display locks of your hair from your very first haircut, don't be embarrassed. It's a "Mom" thing. And besides, who knows? When your hairline starts receding someday, you just might want to ask for them back.

- When she calls you at five o'clock in the morning to say that she doesn't think you're getting enough rest, don't lose any sleep over it. It's a "Mom" thing.

- When you're sick and she makes enough chicken soup to nurse the entire Mayo Clinic, don't let it get you down. It's a "Mom" thing.

- When she still insists on walking you to the school bus (which wouldn't be so bad if you were not the driver now), go with it. It's a "Mom" thing.

And finally, when she shows your baby picture to everyone she meets, just smile. Sure, it's 16" x 20" and you're afraid she'll throw out her back by hauling it around in that solid oak frame, but it's a "Mom" thing—and it's bigger than both of you.

An Age-Old Problem

T HE OTHER DAY my niece asked me about the "olden" days.

"The 'olden' days?" I repeated, glaring.

"Yeah," she continued, exercising little prudence and pressing her luck to the absolute limit. "You know, the olden days... back when you were a little girl."

She didn't have to say another word. I knew precisely where she was heading—right out of my will.

After all, I'm not *that* old. You can't heat a three-bedroom house with my birthday candles or anything like that. (OK, maybe a small condo.) All in all, though, I wouldn't classify myself as being from the "olden" days.

True, I am from a different era. I'm from a time when wearing baggy pants meant you'd put on Grandpa's britches by mistake, not that you were in style. I'm from that grand time when a hundred dollars bought a washing machine instead of tennis shoes.

But my niece's question wasn't totally out of line. The years haven't been kind to me. My crow's feet are a size twelve, I've got laugh lines that extend down to my ankles, and lately my muscles have been sagging more than the economy.

I could try taking a few years off my age by dressing a little younger. But it's not that easy finding orthopedic Spandex shorts or mini-skirts to match my Supp-hose.

I could work on acting younger, too. I could take up skateboarding and roller-blading. I could lower my van windows and drive down the street blasting my radio—that is, if I could find some easy listening tunes with plenty of bass.

If I did all that, my niece wouldn't dare ask me about the "olden" days again. She'd have to totally reassess her opinion of me. I'd show a new spring in my walk, extra pep in my pace, and more get-up-and-go in my gait.

On second thought... a nap sounds even better.

This Little Candle of Mine

B LACKOUTS can be frightening (unless they happen during dinner at my house and you can't see what you're eating).

The town I live in tends to be a bit windy at times, and the wind sometimes triggers power failures. This is exactly what happened one night while my family and I were on the twenty-eighth minute of *60 Minutes.*

"Is it dark in here to the rest of you, or did I just go blind?" I asked, cautiously maneuvering my way to the light switch.

"It's another blackout," my husband's voice echoed through the darkness.

I flicked the switch, but nothing happened.

"It must be the wind again," he said.

"How hard is it blowing?"

"Its usual," he replied as an uprooted eucalyptus tree flew by the window. "We'd better get out the candles. Any idea where they are?"

"The same place they were during the last blackout," I answered.

"Where's that?"

"Wal-Mart. We never bought any."

"Well," he said, "there must be something around here that we could roll up and use as a torch."

I handed him a stack of our bills.

"Sweetheart," he said, "we only need a two-hour torch, not the eternal flame!"

Luckily, for our creditors at least, the silhouette of one of our sons appeared in the doorway, holding what appeared to be the remains of an old birthday candle.

"Perfect!" my husband exclaimed as he grabbed the splinter of wax and quickly lit it.

After looking around for something to set it in (we finally settled on a Twinkie), I began to realize what it must have been like for our forefathers. They had to do everything without electricity. They didn't have light bulbs, fax machines, video games, or VCRs. They had to rough it, and they survived.

About that time, though, the power came back on and everyone resumed watching television. Everyone but me, that is.

As I watched our little candle flickering vainly beneath the fluorescent lights, I could feel that pioneer spirit welling up inside me. I thought to myself, who needs progress? We could live just like our ancestors, without modern conveniences and astronomical utility bills.

I quickly surveyed all the electric gadgets in our home. For lighting, we could use kerosene lamps. Instead of watching television, we could read... what were those things called? Oh yeah, books. As for the washing machine, I could go to the river and beat our clothes against a rock. (If I accidently ripped them in the knees, they'd be in style anyway.) I was absolutely convinced we could make it without the comforts of modern technology.

But when I glanced over at my microwave, I knew I had to reassess my plan. My microwave and I were old friends. I couldn't imagine life without it. I couldn't go back to those days of toiling and sweating in a drive-thru lane for dinner.

I thought for a moment of those pre-Swanson, pre-Lean Cuisine years, then did the only thing I could do—I blew out the candle and ate the Twinkie.

Positively
Negative

T HE WORLD has more than enough negative
people. I'm positive about that. You know the
kind of people I'm speaking of. We've all met them.
No matter what it is, they can always find something negative to say:

At the Grand Canyon
"I've heard of a dog digging holes in your back-yard, but this is ridiculous."

At Graumann's Chinese Theater
"Why didn't they just tell all those movie stars that the cement was wet and make them walk around it?"

At the Great Wall of China
"Chain link would have been a lot cheaper."

At Niagara Falls
"That constant dripping noise is going to keep me up all night."

At the Leaning Tower of Pisa
"I just hope our hotel's in better shape than this."

At Old Faithful
"Big deal. Our sprinkler does the same thing, and I'm not charging tourists to see it."

In front of the Venus de Milo
"Isn't he even going to finish it?"

At the Sistine Chapel
"If my kid ever painted on our ceiling, I'd ground him."

At Mount Rushmore
"He couldn't just carve his initials on a tree like everyone else?"

At the Washington Monument

"If only they had built two of these, we could have played horseshoes."

At the foot of Big Ben

"So when does the cuckoo bird come out?"

In front of the Mona Lisa

"He could have at least waited until she quit laughing to paint her!"

I can't help but feel sorry for negative people. They miss so much in life. They positively do.

Black-Tie Baseball

THE MOTHER of three sons, I've spent a good portion of my life on Little League fields. I've seen it all—from parents blocking the base line with their tripods and video cameras to eight-year-olds taking a nap on the pitcher's mound.

One T-ball game in particular stands out in my memory. It was the final one of the season, and I wouldn't have missed it for anything. Unfortunately, though, I was also scheduled that same Saturday to attend a farewell dinner party for a close friend. I knew I wouldn't have time to go home and change after the game, so I decided to come to the baseball field already dressed in my formal evening attire.

Ignoring the stares and telling myself how much my son was going to appreciate this, I held my head high as I walked across the ballpark in my royal blue sequined dress and high heels and took a seat on the bleachers.

At about 5:30, however, the umpire decided the other team was going to be a "no show" and awarded us an automatic win. That was great for our record but not much fun, so the kids asked us parents if we'd stay and play a few innings with them.

Before I could take off my pearls, I was tossed a mitt and instructed to go to centerfield. I have to admit I felt more like an outfield hostess than a ballplayer, but I wanted to be a good sport. I rolled up my sleeves, tied a team jacket around my waist, crammed an entire package of Big League Chew in my mouth, and readied myself for any ball that should fly, roll, or bounce in my direction.

I didn't have to wait long because the very first batter hit a fly ball straight to me. I ran up to it, held out my mitt, and ducked. By the time I looked up again, the runner had already passed second base and was headed for third.

"Throw it to me!" shouted the third baseman.

"Throw it to *me!*" countered the catcher, even louder.

I was so confused. I didn't know which one to throw it to, so I rolled it between them. I figured whichever one wanted it the most could go for it.

We somehow managed to get our turn at bat, but by then, the other side was aware of my baseball prowess. When I stepped up to the plate, all the outfielders took a break and went to the snack bar, but I didn't allow it to shake me. After all, this was T-ball. Even *I* could hit a home run in T-ball.

I adjusted my nylons, pulled my pearls to one side, and took my first swing. It flew straight toward the third baseman. ("It" being the bat, not the ball.)

"Strike one!" the umpire barked.

My next swing missed the ball but hit the umpire squarely in the shin.

"Strike two!" he cried, grabbing his rapidly swelling leg.

This was my last chance. I concentrated. I prayed. I swung and hit a line drive to centerfield. With my high heels rototilling the baseline, I ran as fast as I could toward first. The centerfielder retrieved the ball and threw it in for the easy out. It was obvious the only way I had a chance to make it would be to slide. So down I went. (To this day, the sequins can still be found in the trees around that park.)

It was a noble try, but the umpire called me out.

By the end of the game, I was bruised and limping,

and I smelled like a dugout. I had more runs in my nylons than our team got in the whole game.

With barely twenty minutes to spare, I hobbled over to my car and rushed to my dinner engagement. As soon as I arrived, I went straight to the ladies' lounge, dusted the dirt from my dress, recombed my hair, splashed on some perfume, then joined the party. I figured there was no way anyone could possibly tell I had just spent the last two hours playing a game of T-ball. Unless, of course, they guessed it when my teacup kept slipping out of my mitt...

"When I said this would be our first formal game,
I just meant that the score was going to count."

The Ultimate Birthday Gift

MY HUSBAND's fortieth birthday was fast approaching, and I wanted to buy him a special gift.

He didn't need another pair of glow-in-the-dark pajamas. The glow from his last pair was already keeping the neighbors awake at night. Another tie didn't sound very exciting, either. He already owned one shaped like a trout, one with little flashing lights, and one that played "Home, Home on the Range" whenever you pressed the buffalo head in the center. Buying him another home repair manual was out of the question, too—especially since we were still paying for the repairs of all the repairs he'd already made around the house.

So, what did he want for his big 4-0? A new fishing pole? New house slippers? A better eraser for his golf game?

"What I'd really like is a body scan," he said one evening when the subject came up.

"A body scan?"

He nodded. "You know, where they put you into that big machine and look inside at all your vital organs."

"But wouldn't a sports blooper video be a lot more entertaining?" I asked.

"Go ahead and scoff," he said, "but I just heard about a perfectly healthy forty-two year old who died running to the four o'clock bus."

"Heart attack?"

"No, he ran in front of the 3:55 bus. But my point is, why take chances?"

"But without any symptoms, our insurance won't cover a full body scan," I explained. "It could run into thousands of dollars."

"Maybe we can put it on our Diners Club card," he

said while taking his pulse... again. "Or we could have the scan done in stages. That way, the expense won't hit all at once."

"Let me see if I've got this right," I said with just a hint of sarcasm. "You want me to sign up for the 'X-ray of the Month Club'?"

"And I should get an EKG while I'm at it, too," he added, with his hand pressed against his chest, on guard for any irregular heartbeats.

"But why?" I asked, puzzled. "The one you took last week was normal, wasn't it?"

"Yes," he said. "But I'd like to get a second opinion."

"That *was* a second opinion."

"And I'd better have my cholesterol level checked."

"You just checked it two weeks ago. It was perfect."

"That was before I heard about the lady who went in for a routine cholesterol check and ended up in the ICU."

"Because of her cholesterol?"

"So bad, it clogged the needle. And I'm worried about my blood pressure, too."

"You don't have high blood pressure," I reminded him.

"Not yet," he agreed. "But if I'm only checking it eight times a day on my digital blood pressure monitor, maybe I'm missing it."

"Look," I said. "It's good to be concerned about

your health, and early detection does save lives, but you really do need to lighten up."

He couldn't say a word. He was busy checking his tonsils in a pocket mirror and the tongue depressor was in the way. So I continued.

"Try being more like me. I'm getting older, too, you know, but I don't spend my day fretting over my blood pressure. I'm comfortable with the fact that the nurse checked it last week and it was just fine. Of course, I was talking to her at the time. She could have misread the results. And I don't worry about my cholesterol level either. My doctor said I was well within the normal range. But then again, that *was* last week. I've had several bags of potato chips since then. Come to think of it, I've had several bags of potato chips since breakfast! I don't even worry about gallstones, although, I did hear about a man who grew a stone so big, it rolled over and nearly crushed his tapeworm."

I paused for a brief moment, then picked up the telephone. "On second thought, dear, I think I will call the doctor. Maybe he's running a two-for-one special."

Blessed Insurance

A S PARENT sponsors of our church's youth group, my husband and I assist the youth council in planning their monthly activities. At a recent meeting, however, things got a little out of hand.

"Who wants to go white water rafting?" the president asked, beaming with excitement.

Every hand but ours shot up. (My husband is

prone to motion sickness, and I still wear an inflatable duck ring in a Jacuzzi. There was no way rafting was going to get our votes.)

"White water rafting?" I said. "Don't you realize you'd be risking your lives?"

"No more than when we eat your brownies at youth bake sales," the secretary pointed out.

She had me there.

"Or we could go hot air ballooning," the vice-president suggested.

"Aw-Right!" the council shouted, exchanging high fives.

While they excitedly discussed the certain fun and adventure of hot air ballooning, my husband and I sat there in sheer amazement. Teenagers today are fearless. But then, I suppose they have to be. How else could they face their closets day in and day out?

"Look," I coaxed. "Why don't we plan something where we keep our feet on the ground—you know, like roller skating?"

The treasurer quickly pointed out that he had seen me roller skate, and my feet didn't spend much time on the ground with that sport, either.

"Let's go parasailing," the secretary submitted.

"Parasailing?" I echoed, recalling a distinct aversion to heights. "Is that scriptural?"

"The Bible doesn't say, 'Thou shalt not parasail'" the treasurer assured me.

"But parasailing's so dangerous," I said, quickly checking through the concordance myself.

"The guides are experts and tell you everything you need to know. All you have to do is remember to follow their instructions," the president insisted.

I thought to myself, isn't this the same kid who forgot his Bible four Sundays in a row, left his jacket at the winter youth retreat, and locked his keys in his car last Friday night?

"Why don't we go water skiing instead?" I suggested.

"Hey, yeah, that's even better," agreed the secretary. "And afterwards, we'll go cliff diving."

"Cool!" was the rest of the council's response.

"The pastor will never approve of cliff diving," I declared.

"Sure he will," the president said confidently. "We'll tell him you're jumping first."

Recalling all the times I had roasted our pastor at banquets and meetings, I figured the president just may have had a point.

The more they talked about their latest proposal, the more it became obvious that my husband and I were not youth sponsor material.

As soon as we could, we quietly slipped out of the room and joined the seniors meeting down the hall.

"This'll be more our speed," my husband assured me as we entered the room. "We can help them plan croquet parties, shuffleboard competitions, and horse-shoe tournaments. Why, there'll be no end to the excitement."

We sat in the back and listened as their leader continued making his announcements.

"Now, don't forget to mark those dates on your calendars," he said. "This coming Saturday, due to popular demand, we'll be going skydiving again, and the following Friday is our bungee jumping outing."

Skydiving? Bungee jumping? I looked at my husband. He looked at me. Without uttering a single word, we both stood up, slipped out of the room, and rushed back to the youth... where it was safe.

26

To Love, Honor, and Cherish... Even While on Vacation

I 'VE HEARD it said many couples have their worst disagreements while on vacation. A few times my husband and I have begun ours before we've even pulled out of the driveway. More often than not, it's over something trivial like who locked the keys in the trunk of the car, who packed the map in the bottom of the cooler, and why are we taking twelve suitcases when we're only staying overnight?

Men, in general, don't understand the need to rent a U-Haul trailer for a weekend trip to the mountains. They're embarrassed when Amtrak has to add on an extra car just for their family's luggage. They get annoyed when airplanes have to fly at lower altitudes because of the weight of their wife's overnight bag. In short, they don't understand the importance of traveling prepared.

Women, on the other hand, know how to pack. I myself just make a list of those items I know for sure I'm *not* going to need, then simply load up the rest of the house.

Another cause of vacation stress is the "Did you remember to?" blues. There are so many last minute things that need to be done before leaving on a vacation that it's inevitable you will forget a few—not one of which will enter your consciousness until you're at least one hundred miles away from home and making good time. Then, all of a sudden, you'll remember you forgot to turn off the sprinklers in the front yard, you forgot to cancel the paper, and you forgot one (or more) of the kids. And since you don't want your yard flooded, your papers flying through your windows when you're not home, and your kids making *Home Alone* seem like "Romper Room," you do the only thing you can do—you turn around and head back.

I can't recall a single vacation where we haven't had to turn around and go back. In fact, on most of our trips we've ended up doing more backtracking than a politician.

The video-happy spouse also causes vacation discord. He'll either tape you while you're napping (the nerve of him interrupting your driving like that) or while you're eating. Just as you're about to take a bite the size of Rhode Island, he'll zoom in for a dramatic close-up of your tonsils. (I've had several close-ups taken of my opened mouth, and I don't appreciate it in the least... especially when they're later confused with footage of the Grand Canyon.)

The "I'm not lost, they must have moved to Albuquerque" spouse is the type of person who refuses to look at a map or stop and ask directions. You know the scene:

"Uh, dear... I think we've lost Interstate 40."

"Why do you say that, sweetheart?"

"Well, for one thing, didn't it used to be paved?"

Without a doubt, though, the leading cause of the vacation dispute has got to be the rest stop. That's because rest stops are like army induction physicals. Nobody will ever need to go in until after he or she has passed one.

Even with the little disagreements, though, vacations are still an important part of family life. They can provide us with terrific lifelong memories if we can only remember to relax and have fun, enjoy the scenery and each other, and leave the constant eruptions to the geysers at Yellowstone.

Hospital Visitors Can Be Hazardous to Your Health

FLORENCE Nightingale, I'm not.

The patients I visit usually end up bribing the hospital operator to announce visiting hours are over twenty minutes ahead of schedule.

My problem is I try too hard to show my concern. I've hugged patients and accidentally pulled out their IV tubing. I've knocked over water pitchers while trying to hand patients a drink. I've brought fudge to a diabetic, spring flowers to an allergy sufferer, and the morning newspaper to a person with a heart condition.

Still, hospital visitation is an important ministry. That's why I've decided to pass along the following tips on what *not* to do while visiting the infirm.

When making hospital visits...

- Never discuss the rising cost of medical care while the patient is having her blood pressure taken.

- Never tell a patient in a full-body cast to "hang loose."

- Never ask the patient to keep down his moaning so you can hear the television set.

- Never mistake the patient's X-rays for a map of the L.A. freeway system.

- Never ask the patient to scoot over so you can get in a short nap yourself.

- Never hang your purse on the leg of a patient in traction.

- Never tell a patient that you just saw her doctor coloring in the cafeteria.

- Never tease a patient by telling him you think you see a crack in his IV bottle.

- Never fluff a pillow while the patient is still on it.

- Never look at a patient's stitches unless you are positioned to faint away from his dinner tray.

- Giving the patient a shave is a thoughtful gesture. However, never unplug his EKG to plug in the electric razor.

- Never give the patient a gift cookbook entitled *101 Ways to Prepare Lime Gelatin*.

- Never raise both the head of the bed and the foot of the bed at the same time. (Unless it's time for the patient's evening shot and he's trying to hide from his nurses.)

- Never tell a patient who's had chicken broth for six days how the steak and lobster you ate for dinner gave you indigestion.

- Never tie more than one helium balloon bouquet to the patient's bed. (I did this once, and it took the hospital staff two-and-a-half hours to get the patient down from the ceiling.)

- Never tell the patient every little detail of your own surgical experiences—unless his sleeping pills aren't working and his doctor requests it.

And finally, never visit unless it's during regular visiting hours. If the convalescing patient has friends and family waking him up at all sorts of ridiculous hours just to ask how he's feeling, what are his nurses going to have left to do for fun?

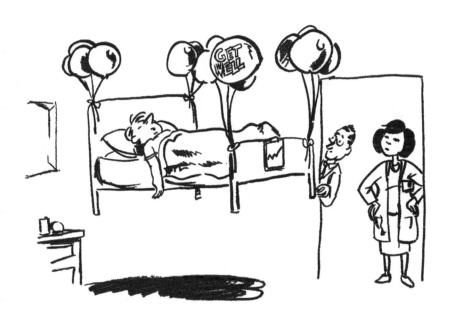

"Maybe balloon bouquets weren't
such a good idea after all."

Isn't It Romantic?

WHEN IT COMES to romance, my husband is much more demonstrative than I am. He holds me tightly in his arms... especially when we're passing a half-price sale in progress. He leaves loving little notes in my purse. I leave notes in his wallet, too. Just last night I wrote, "My love is a garden, you are the sun. I took the twenty and left the one." And at least once a week he takes me out for a cozy dinner for two by candlelight. Not only does he go to all the trouble of reserving our special booth at McDonald's, but he even gets written permission from the manager to light the candle.

I may not go to such extremes when showing my love, but I do plenty of other amorous things. I play soft, romantic music every night. (It's not my fault he can't hear it over the smoke alarm going off in the kitchen.) On special occasions I like to dab a little expensive perfume behind each ear. (When it mixes with the Ben Gay fumes rising from my shoulders, I'm nothing short of irresistible.) I believe in dressing romantically, too. All my flannel pajamas have little hearts on them, and my reindeer houseslippers are both winking. And when my husband came home the other night, I greeted him dressed from head to toe in romantic lace. (All right, on my way to the door I tripped over a dining room chair and got tangled up in the tablecloth, but he didn't know that.)

Still, whether the lights are turned up or turned down, whether he's whispering sweet nothings in my ear or asking if I paid the Visa bill, whether we're listening to Sinatra or the rap album that's blaring from our son's room, we both realize how important it is to keep the romance alive in a marriage. After all, it's the honeymoon that should be lasting a lifetime, not just the payments on it.

Things Left Behind

THE OTHER DAY I passed an estate sale. The deceased had died in her late eighties, and her surviving sister was selling all her late sister's belongings.

I have to admit it was a bit depressing seeing a near-century of living reduced to three or four folding tables of various knick-knacks, clothes, dishes, and books.

As carload after carload of curious shoppers stopped to search for that bargain of a lifetime, I couldn't help but wonder about the things I might be leaving behind someday. Who would be getting all of my valued belongings? I began to make a list:

- I'll leave my telephone to my teenage son. The executor of my estate wouldn't be able to separate it from his ear without surgery, anyway.

- I'll donate my desk to a local college. Perhaps some poor, struggling student needs a place to take his naps, too.

- I'll leave all my financial holdings to Congress. They're already used to working with deficits.

- I'll leave my recipes to *Ripley's Believe It or Not.*

- I'll leave my savings account to my paperboy. That is, unless he doesn't want the extra fourteen bucks bumping him into a higher income tax bracket.

- I'll leave my VCR to my two-year-old nephew. Maybe he can figure out how to program it.

- I'll leave my Picasso to an art museum. It was painted by Biff Picasso and a few of the numbers show through, but a museum still might take it.

- I'll leave the Smithsonian first edition copies of all my books (as they have already requested). They said they could use them to prop up the other exhibits.

I could have gone on and on, but I didn't really see the need. After all, these were only material goods. The most valuable possessions anyone can pass to another generation are those things which can't be written down in a will. They can only be left behind in the hearts of our loved ones—inner strength, a giving heart, the ability to laugh, and the knowledge that no matter what comes up in this life, God is there to get us through it.

Other Books of Interest from Servant Publications

A House of Many Blessings
A Christian Guide to Hospitality
Quin Sherrer and Laura Watson

Many people might think that hospitality requires gourmet cooking, elegant decorating, and lots of money. It doesn't. Quin and Laura want to give readers a vision of the tremendous value of ordinary, down-dome Christian hospitality and how it can bless and strengthen God's people. **$8.99**

Finding Friendship with God
Floyd McClung

Floyd McClung reveals the barriers that prevent Christians from enjoying God and teaches them how to talk with him, to rely on his friendship every day, to listen to him, and to grow in understanding him. *Finding Friendship with God* whets our appetite for this most intimate and satisfying love relationship. **$8.99**

How to Survive Practically Anything
Dr. Dan Montgomery

Dr. Dan Montgomery believes that Christians can learn how to survive practically any tragedy they experience in life. He teaches readers how to respect and work through their emotions, listen to what their bodies are saying, allow their minds to be renewed, find reliable support, and surrender to God's loving care. **$8.99**

Available at your Christian bookstore or from:
Servant Publications • Dept. 209 • P.O. Box 7455
Ann Arbor, Michigan 48107
Please include payment plus $2.75 per book
for postage and handling.
*Send for our FREE catalog of Christian
books, music, and cassettes.*